the little book of CHINESE HOROSCOPES

First published in 2025 by OH
An Imprint of HEADLINE PUBLISHING GROUP

1

Disclaimer:

This book is intended for general informational purposes only and should not be relied upon as recommending or promoting any specific practice, diet or method of treatment. It is not intended to diagnose, advise, treat or prevent any illness or condition and is not a substitute for advice from a professional practitioner of the subject matter contained in this book. You should not use the information in this book as a substitute for medication, nutritional, diet, spiritual or other treatment that is prescribed by your practitioner. Furthermore, the publisher is not affiliated with and does not sponsor or endorse any uses of or beliefs about in any way referred in this book.

Cataloguing in Publication Data is available from the British Library

ISBN 978-1-03541-980-7

Compiled and written by: Malcolm Croft
Editorial: Saneaah Muhammad
Designed and typeset in Joanna Sans Nova by: Stephen Cary
Project manager: Russell Porter
Illustrations: Adobe Stock
Production: Arlene Lestrade
Printed and bound in China

Headline's policy is to use papers that are natural, renewable and recyclable products and made from wood grown in well-managed forests and other controlled sources. The logging and manufacturing processes are expected to conform to the environmental regulations of the country of origin.

HEADLINE PUBLISHING GROUP
An Hachette UK Company
Carmelite House, 50 Victoria Embankment, London EC4Y 0DZ

www.headline.co.uk   www.hachette.co.uk

personalities, career, compatibility, marriage and fortune, becoming an essential everyday guide for followers of the zodiac who wish to live as prosperous a life as possible.

Welcome to *The Little Book of Chinese Horoscopes*, a tiny tome for those seeking to advance their astrological aspirations, a compact compendium that will help you learn even more about yourself and your future, as is pre-destined by the universe. The closer you look and the more you learn, the more you'll come to understand why the zodiac is so vital to so many citizens around the world and how you can use that knowledge to power up your precious time here on Earth. Your destiny lives within – let's go find it. Enjoy!

the GREAT RACE

The Chinese zodiac and the astrological importance of the 12 animal signs all began with the **jade emperor's great race**.

According to ancient myth, the Jade Emperor – Chinese culture's primordial creation God – devised an endurance race on Earth to find out which animals would be deserving of a place on the Emperor's lunar calendar.

The race included all the terrain on Earth, including a mighty, but dangerous, river. Whichever animals crossed the finishing line the fastest would be immortalized in the stars forever. Only 12 spots were available in accordance with the 12 new moon cycles that dictate earthly months, and each winner would have a year named after them – a cycle that would repeat every 12 years.

The smallest competitor, the Rat, was the first animal to win the Emperor's Great Race, and takes its place as the first animal in the Chinese zodiac.

RAT

cunning and resourceful

year of the rat:
1924, 1936, 1948, 1960,
1972, 1984, 1996, 2008,
2020, 2032

chinese word: **SHŬ**

motto: **I THINK**

yin/yang: **YIN**

season: **WINTER**

lunar month: **DECEMBER – JANUARY**

ruling hour: **23:00 – 00:59**

western zodiac: **SAGITTARIUS**

positive qualities: charming, cunning, curious

negative qualities: stubborn, competitive, devious

Known for their lightning-fast thinking, the Rat is the representation of resourcefulness in the Chinese zodiac.

Ambitious and resilient, Rats are shrewd enough to always sniff out an opportunity to get ahead faster than anyone else.

Proof that size matters not.

ARE YOU a rat?

You can be clever, adaptable and cunning without breaking a sweat. You can tackle any obstacle or opportunity that presents itself with overwhelming confidence. You can be witty and charming, too, and highly magnetic in large groups, often finding yourself at the centre of attention.

You have a desire to win at all costs which can often make you appear too narrow-minded, but when you create your own success, others tend to follow.

the LUCK of the rat

lucky

numbers: 2 and 3
days: 4th and 13th
colours: blue, gold, green
flower: lily

unlucky

numbers: 5 and 9
colours: yellow, brown

rats IN LOVE

With their great sense of humour and ability to express themselves supremely well, particularly when they perceive themselves to be the smartest in the room, Rats have very little trouble finding a romantic date or mate.

Rats constantly seek excitement – the chase is as important as the catch – and are happy to get their hands dirty in the process.

Of course, Rats are famously fickle and flirty, and they are prone to moving on to the next source of entertainment if they lose interest, giving rise to the term "love rat".

PERFECT MATCH

For deep love connections, Rats find themselves most at ease with Dragons, Monkeys and Oxen, uniting in harmony with their magical magnetism and quickfire charm.

For close friendships, Rats should seek out Pigs, Tigers and Dogs.

Horses and Goats – beware of the Rat. Their love of their own voice may become a little too much burden for you to bear.

rats AT WORK

Eager to lead and please, Rats tend to be highly skilled and highly competitive. While Rats may often lack courage and discretion, they are forever the first to take advantage of a situation.

Their keen sense of judgement is second-to-none, a quality that helps them foresee problems in the workplace before they arise.

Of all the Chinese zodiac animals, Rats are attracted to money the most and tend to be the most prosperous and wealthy. However, that comes at a cost: Rats are thrifty and cautious to part with their hard-earned wealth.

rats in their ELEMENT

Wood Rat (1924, 1984)
Creative, adaptable, diplomatic

Fire Rat (1936, 1996)
Energetic, passionate, ambitious

Earth Rat (1948, 2008)
Practical, reliable, hardworking

Metal Rat (1960, 2020)
Determined, ambitious, disciplined

Water Rat (1972, 2032)
Intelligent, adaptable, intuitive

the GREAT RACE

Size doesn't matter when it comes to the Rat, the smallest entrant in the Emperor's Race. Knowing it wasn't the strongest or fastest among the 12 animals, the Rat used its quick thinking to convince the Ox to carry it on its back across the mighty river near the finishing line.

The strong Ox, being kind and reliable, agreed. As the Ox reached the other side, the Rat leapt off the Ox's back and dashed to the finish line to claim first place... without ever thanking the Ox.

Pure Rat.

NOTABLE rats

Eminem, 1972

Prince Harry, 1984

Ozzy Osbourne, 1948

Zendaya, 1996

Tim Cook, 1960

King Charles III, 1948

LeBron James, 1984

Dwayne Johnson, 1972

Bono, 1960

Scarlett Johansson, 1984

rats in their
OWN WORDS

"We make guilty of our disasters the sun, the moon and stars, as if we were villains on necessity, fools by heavenly compulsion; knaves, thieves and treachers, by spherical predominance."

William Shakespeare
King Lear, Act 1, Scene 2, 1606.

"As human beings, we suffer from an innate tendency to jump to conclusions, to judge people too quickly and to pronounce them failures or heroes without due consideration."

King Charles III
in a foreword to a biography of
King George III, 1972.

YEAR of the CAT

"I have lived with several
Zen masters – all of them cats."

Eckhart Tolle
*The Power of Now: A Guide to Spiritual
Enlightenment*, 1997.

There is no year of the Cat in the Chinese zodiac, despite Cats, especially waving ones, being a symbol of good fortune in the nation's astrology-inspired culture.

The reason for this is simple: the Rat.

At the start of the Great Race, the Cat and the Rat were great friends. However, the Cat's love of sleeping overcame the Cat, though not without first asking the Rat to wake it up before the race began. But the cunning Rat did not, and the Cat slept in, missing the race.

By the time the Cat woke up, the race was over. The Rat had won.

OX

dependable and patient

year of the ox:
1925, 1937, 1949, 1961,
1973, 1985, 1997, 2009,
2021, 2033

chinese word: **NIÚ**

motto: **I WORK HARD**

yin/yang: **YIN**

season: **WINTER**

lunar month: **JANUARY – FEBRUARY**

ruling hour: **01:00 – 02:59**

western zodiac: **TAURUS**

positive traits: strong, dependable, serious

negative traits: narrow-minded, slow, unable to express themselves

Reliable and patient, Oxen are the strong, silent type.

We all have that Ox in our life that we depend upon.

The only thing standing in the way of an Ox is none other than the Ox itself: their stubborn determination makes them slow to progress. But with it brings unparalleled precision and power.

ARE YOU an ox?

You can be diligent, dependable and determined. You can be stoic and unflashy, a person who can endure pain or hardship without showing their feelings or complaining.

Working hard and smart are the keys to your success, as well as not being influenced by others' opinions.

Sure, you can be a stick-in-the-mud sometimes and cling too seriously to rules, but due to your size and strength (not to mention stubbornness), no one is going to force you to be anything else.

the LUCK of the ox

lucky

numbers: 1 and 4

days: 13th and 27th

colours: white, yellow, green

flowers: tulip, peach blossom

unlucky

numbers: 5 and 6

colour: blue

oxen IN LOVE

Underneath an Ox's calm, cool exterior lies a brooding and passionate intensity – especially toward Roosters and Snakes!

What Oxen may lack in romance and sparkling conversation, they make up for in strong ideals, devotion and fidelity.

You'll never find an Ox far from home; their castle is their keep. In the right mood, an Ox will let down their guard and show their trusted partners their gentleness and affection. When they do, it's deep and oh-so-powerful.

PERFECT MATCH

Oxen are committed to the ones they love. Love connections with Horses and Goats can lead to conflict, so they are best avoided.

An Ox will find true companionship with Dogs, Rabbits, Tigers and particularly Monkeys: their playfulness offers a complementary counterbalance to an Ox's seriousness.

oxen AT WORK

The indispensable powerhouse of any workplace, Oxen are productive as they have the innate ability to endure hardships and challenges that others cannot.

As the symbol of hard work in Chinese culture, Oxen struggle to understand the meaning of giving up, instead possessing a responsible and determined attitude towards work much greater than other animal signs.

oxen in their ELEMENT

Wood Ox (1925, 1985)
Decisive, straightforward, protective

Fire Ox (1937, 1997)
Practical, short-sighted, narrow-minded

Earth Ox (1949, 2009)
Honest, responsible, prudent

Metal Ox (1961, 2021)
Active, popular, quiet

Water Ox (1973, 2033)
Reliable, patient, strong sense of justice

the GREAT RACE

Known for its determination, the Ox was confident in its ability to cross the mighty river of the Great Race, despite its swift power.

However, as the Ox reached the other side of the river, the opportune rat, true to its nature, leapt off the Ox's back and claimed first place, despite the Ox having done most of the hard work!

The Rat may have won the race, but the Ox's dependable values remained intact.

NOTABLE oxen

Barack Obama, 1961

Rosa Parks, 1913

Margeret Thatcher, 1925

Walt Disney, 1901

Bruce Springsteen, 1949

Princess Diana, 1961

Malcolm X, 1925

Kylie Jenner, 1997

Meryl Streep, 1949

Gal Gadot, 1985

oxen in their
OWN WORDS

"The future rewards those who press on. I don't have time to feel sorry for myself. I don't have time to complain. I'm going to press on."

Barack Obama

in a Black Caucus speech at
the White House, September 24, 2011.

"I do things differently, because I don't go by a rule book. I lead from the heart, not the head, and that's got me into trouble in my work."

Princess Diana

interview with *BBC Panorama*, November 20, 1995.

TIGER

brave and adventurous

year of the tiger:
1926, 1938, 1950, 1962,
1974, 1986, 1998, 2010,
2022, 2034

chinese word: **HŬ**

motto: **I AM BRAVE**

yin/yang: **YANG**

season: **SPRING**

lunar month: **FEBRUARY – MARCH**

ruling hour: **03:00 – 04:59**

western zodiac: **AQUARIUS**

positive qualities: courageous, assertive, optimistic

negative qualities: impetuous, reckless, stubborn

In Chinese folklore, the Tiger is the king of animals, as is befitting of an animal with such elegance, courage and agility.

Tigers are fearless and dominating leaders that are always ready to pounce on a big risk if it is worth taking.

ARE YOU a tiger?

You love being at the centre of the action and attention, a typical trait of Tigers.

You were born to lead and are highly respected by peers for your skills to take control of a situation when others wilt into the background.

Yes, you can be unpredictable, reckless and stubborn, especially when forced to relinquish power, but you're able to express your emotions in an authoritative manner and take bold action no matter how uncertain you may be of the outcome.

the LUCK of the tiger

lucky

numbers: 1 and 3

days: 16th and 27th

colours: blue, grey, orange

flowers: yellow lily, cineraria

unlucky

numbers: 6, 7 and 8

colour: brown

tigers IN LOVE

Tigers love to be loved and are always on the prowl for their feelings to be requited.

Tigers often seek a shoulder to cry on when necessary but hate to be thought of as a burden.

Tigers make excellent friends, particularly with Rabbits, Dragons and Roosters, not only for their emotional acumen but also for their ability to express themselves no matter how unpopular the opinion.

Snakes and Monkeys, stay away – your style over substance is not welcome here.

PERFECT MATCH

In love and relationships, Tigers are predominantly on the lookout for Horses, Dogs and Pigs.

Only these animals reflect the values of fierce loyalty and courage that a Tiger seeks in themselves.

tigers AT WORK

Courageous and charismatic, Tigers fearlessly pursue their goals and inspire others to follow. That said, a Tiger's impulsiveness can often lead to reckless behaviour, especially if they're trying to prove someone wrong or impress them.

A Tiger is excellent at spotting problems but less able to see the solutions, leading to leaping into action before considering the consequences of their actions.

As the saying goes, "Whatever you do, don't tread on a Tiger's tail" – this goes for Tigers even more so at work.

tigers in their # ELEMENT

Wood Tiger (1974, 2034)
Compassionate, open, expressive

Fire Tiger (1926, 1986)
Optimistic, independent, zero self-control

Earth Tiger (1938, 1998)
Adventurous, faithful, realistic

Metal Tiger (1950, 2010)
Enthusiastic, indecisive, stubborn

Water Tiger (1962, 2022)
Talented, confident, ignorant

the GREAT RACE

At the start of the race, the Tiger had the confidence and conviction to believe it could win.

The Tiger dived into the mighty river with little regard for its safety and used its powerful paws to push against the harsh current.

Alas, despite its strength, the Tiger soon struggled and grew too tired, allowing the Ox (and the Rat!) to gain the advantage. The Tiger's courage was strong but so too was its thoughtlessness.

If only it had taken the time to think of a better way to cross, it might have won.

NOTABLE tigers

Queen Elizabeth II, 1926

Marilyn Monroe, 1926

Leonardo DiCaprio, 1974

Tom Cruise, 1962

Lady Gaga, 1986

Victoria Beckham, 1974

Bill Murray, 1950

David Attenborough, 1926

Christian Bale, 1974

Usain Bolt, 1986

tigers in their
OWN WORDS

"I've spent most of my life running
away from myself."

Marilyn Monroe
Saturday Evening Post, May 1956.

"I've always been spontaneous and outgoing. I've tried lots of things so I've got some good life experiences, which is great because it means I've got lots of material to work with as an actor."

Leonardo DiCaprio
The Express, September 22, 2002.

ANIMAL TRINES

The 12 animal signs of the Chinese zodiac are made up of four subsections known as **animal trines**.

the first trine includes the Rat, Dragon and Monkey. These are the most powerful, but also the most unpredictable, animals of the zodiac. They are known for their intelligence, charm and wit..

the second trine includes the Ox, Snake and Rooster. They are known for their patience, discipline and reliability.

the third trine includes the Tiger, Horse and Dog. They are known for their adventurous spirit, bravery and idealism.

the fourth trine includes the Rabbit, Goat and Pig. They are known for their gentle, compassionate and nurturing traits.

RABBIT

gentle and patient

year of the rabbit:
1927, 1939, 1951, 1963,
1975, 1987, 1999, 2011,
2023, 2035

chinese word: **TÙ**

motto: **I AM KIND**

yin/yang: **YIN**

season: **SPRING**

lunar month: **MARCH – APRIL**

ruling hour: **05:00 – 06:59**

western zodiac: **PISCES**

positive qualities: polite, intuitive, sensitive

negative qualities: superficial, melancholic, indecisive

Admired for their compassionate approach to life, love and friendships, Rabbits have a strong sense of doing the good and right thing.

Rabbits prefer diplomacy over aggression and seek harmony and peace above all else.

If Rabbits were human, they'd be hop-happy hippies.

ARE YOU a rabbit?

You can be virtuous, kind and reserved – admit it! You can also be trusted among your large and loyal friendship groups. Your friends are perhaps the thing you take most seriously.

You seldom lose your cool and are wise beyond your years, though you're too humble to admit it. You are rarely ever tempted to start a fight or take a side, preferring to negotiate a peace deal.

This makes you a caring referee if sometimes a little meek or submissive. You rarely make yourself the centre of attention but have the social skills to do so effectively when you try.

the LUCK of the rabbit

lucky

numbers: 3, 4 and 6

days: 26th, 27th and 29th

colours: red, pink, purple, blue

flowers: plantain lily, jasmine, snapdragon

unlucky

numbers: 1, 7 and 8

colours: brown, yellow, white

rabbits IN LOVE

In love and life, Rabbits strive for security and a peaceful existence.

All a Rabbit seeks is to live a good life, care-free and full of happiness without all the fuss of gambling with danger and impulse. Rabbits prefer privacy at first, choosing to snuggle in sensuality and affection over hot, burning passion.

It's no surprise that Rabbits love large families – and how you get them! – and ensure that family ties stay strong even if it requires extra effort.

PERFECT MATCH

Rabbits are lovers not fighters. They find romantic solace in the loyal, gentle and compassionate Goats and Dogs first and foremost but have been known to chase the odd Pig!

Rabbits love their friends more than anything else and usually find their close friends to be Tigers, Monkeys and Horses, radiating many of their traits.

Roosters and Rabbits rarely mix well together, and Dragons are best avoided – too much danger.

rabbits AT WORK

Rabbits are the peacemakers in professional settings.

Due to their excellent communication skills and valuing diplomacy over war, Rabbits often serve as mediators, seeing the good in both sides of the argument when any office politics or conflicts arise.

That often means, however, that Rabbits find themselves in the middle of a fight they didn't start. They often become the messengers who get caught in the crossfire when their inability to make a decision reveals itself.

rabbits in their ELEMENT

Wood Rabbit (1975, 2035)
Clever, lively, shrewd

Fire Rabbit (1927, 1987)
Smart, flexible, open

Earth Rabbit (1939, 1999)
Frank, ambitious, reserved

Metal Rabbit (1951, 2011)
Kind-hearted, conservative, enthusiastic

Water Rabbit (1963, 2023)
Gentle, adaptable, meek

the GREAT RACE

Revered for their agility and super-speed, the Rabbit knew that it would quickly hop ahead of the other animals when the Great Race began.

However, as the Rabbit reached the mighty river, it realized it was at a disadvantage by lacking strong swimming skills.

To overcome this, the Rabbit used the river's natural obstacles to its advantage and jumped from stone to stone and log to log until it reached the other side.

The Rabbit then hopped to fourth place!

NOTABLE rabbits

Michael Jordan, 1963

Angelina Jolie, 1975

Albert Einstein, 1879

David Beckham, 1975

Johnny Depp, 1963

Novak Djokovic, 1987

Quentin Tarantino, 1963

Brad Pitt, 1963

Kate Winslet, 1975

Tiger Woods, 1975

rabbits in their
OWN WORDS

"Only a life lived for others
is a life worthwhile."

Albert Einstein
interview with *The New York Times*,
June 20, 1932.

"If you don't know the guy on the other side of the world, love him anyway because he's just like you. He has the same dreams, the same hopes and fears. It's one world, pal. We're all neighbours."

Frank Sinatra
interview with Joe Hyams, *Playboy*, February 1963.

the FIVE ELEMENTS

Chinese zodiac animals are associated with five natural elements – **wood, fire, earth, metal** and **water**.

Every 60 years – five cycles of 12 – these elements rotate, boosting additional zodiacal influences to the characteristics of the animal it is paired with in that year.

WOOD:
Elevates creativity, growth and flexibility

METAL:
Represents strength, determination and resilience

FIRE:
Represents passion, energy and assertiveness

WATER:
Symbolizes wisdom, intuition and adaptability

EARTH:
Symbolizes stability, practicality and nurturing qualities

DRAGON

magnetic and majestic

year of the dragon:
1928, 1940, 1952, 1964,
1976, 1988, 2000, 2012,
2024, 2036

chinese word: LÒNG

motto: I AM POWERFUL

yin/yang: YANG

season: SPRING

lunar month: APRIL–MAY

ruling hour: 07:00–08:59

western zodiac: ARIES

positive qualities: powerful, fortunate, noble

negative qualities: quick-tempered, mysterious, arrogant

The only mythical creature in Eastern astrology, the Dragon also happens to be the most powerful of all the animal signs.

The Dragon is revered in national folklore for its nobility, luck and imagination.

ARE YOU a dragon?

You can be confident, dedicated and always strive to be successful in all you do. You can also be full of a restless energy burdened by a non-stop desire to live the biggest life possible.

While that can become tiresome for others – in particular, Dogs! – other Dragons will find your dynamism attractive.

You don't like routines, boredom or anything inside the ordinary and are constantly trying out new projects, places and people, especially if they inspire you to push your passions to the extreme. Fortune favours the bold, and none are more bold than the Dragon.

the LUCK of the dragon

lucky

numbers: 1, 6 and 7

days: 1st and 16th

colours: gold, silver

flowers: bleeding-heart glory bower, dragon flowers

unlucky

numbers: 3 and 8

colours: blue, green

dragons IN LOVE

Dragons require a love partner equally as exciting, mysterious and fun-loving as themselves.

Dragons need wings to fly, and all romantic interests must keep up with their exotic flights of fancy if they are to retain its interest.

Ultimately, a Dragon's love connection must be adventurous enough to keep their attention. Dogs and Rabbits – you're too sensible and grounded to stop a magical Dragon from flying away.

PERFECT MATCH

A dragon knows how to live and love life. They often find that their preferred long-term companions are Rats, Monkeys and Roosters – creatures just as curious as they are.

You'll see that Dragons find their best friends in courageous adventurers such as Tigers, Snakes and Horses.

dragons AT WORK

Dragons are born leaders. They are capable of inspiring and influencing greatness within others with their high-flying imagination and desire to do something new, bold and original.

However, with all this great power comes great ego, pride and arrogance, and Dragons find even the most minor of criticism, feedback or even teamwork too much to take.

The potential for Dragons to start conflict at work is greater when they fly a little too close to the sun for their own good – and are told to come back down to Earth.

dragons in their ELEMENT

Wood Dragon (1964, 2024)
Introverted, cautious, fickle

Fire Dragon (1976, 2036)
Smart, agile, flexible

Earth Dragon (1928, 1988)
Ambitious, hardworking, tiresome

Metal Dragon (1940, 2000)
Virtuous, straightforward, talented

Water Dragon (1952, 2012)
Determined, vigorous, naive

the GREAT RACE

The Jade Emperor expected the Dragon –
the only winged mythical creature – to win
the Great Race easily. However, the Dragon,
even with its great speed and power, chose not
to win.

As soon as the race started, the dragon saw a
nearby village on fire. The Dragon stopped to
blow his icy breath into the sky to help create
rain to douse the flames. Only once the rain
began to fall and the villagers found safety did
the Dragon attend to the race.

The Dragon is an iconic symbol of Chinese
people because of its noble and altruistic
actions during the Great Race.

NOTABLE dragons

Adele, 1988

Keanu Reeves, 1964

John Lennon, 1940

Che Guevara, 1928

Bruce Lee, 1940

Robert Oppenheimer, 1904

Pelé, 1940

Maya Angelou, 1928

Emma Stone, 1988

Roald Dahl, 1916

dragons in their
OWN WORDS

"Do not pray for an easy life,
pray for the strength to endure
a difficult one."

Bruce Lee
Tao of Jeet Kune Do, 1975.

"Without courage we cannot practice any other virtue with consistency. We can't be kind, true, merciful, generous or honest."

Maya Angelou
USA Today, March 5, 1988.

YEAR
of the
DRAGON

In Chinese culture, the **dragon** is the most prized zodiac sign.

People born in the year of the Dragon are destined to find luck, success and wealth.

As a result, in 2024 (the most recent year of the Dragon), China saw a staggering five per cent increase in the number of babies born throughout the year.

> "Dragons are fire made flesh. And fire is power."

Daenerys Targaryen,
A Song of Ice and Fire, George R. R. Martin, 1996.

SNAKE

courageous and curious

year of the snake:
1929, 1941, 1953, 1965,
1977, 1989, 2001, 2013,
2025, 2037

chinese word: **SHÉ**

motto: **I AM WISE**

yin/yang: **YIN**

season: **SUMMER**

lunar month: **MAY–JUNE**

ruling hour: **09:00–10:59**

western zodiac: **TAURUS**

positive qualities: intuitive, charming, glamorous

negative qualities: lazy, greedy, vain

Also known as a mini-Dragon, the Snake, in astrological terms, shares many of the same virtues (and vices) as the Dragon.

It too is wise, enigmatic and powerful. It too is a little too charming for its own good!

However, as the saying goes, "If you've got it, flaunt it", and Snakes have got charm by the basket load.

ARE YOU a snake?

You can be wise and a great thinker. You can be independent and intuitive. You are not one to be rushed into making a decision, big or small.

While Snakes are famed for being perhaps the most attractive of all the astrological animals, with great beauty comes great vanity, and Snakes are also considered the most vain creature.

Thankfully, your beauty will help you find the finer things in life as only the best is good enough for a Snake!

the LUCK of the snake

lucky

numbers: 2, 8 and 9

days: 1st and 23rd

colours: black, red, yellow

flowers: orchid, cactus

unlucky

numbers: 1, 6 and 7

colours: brown, gold, white

snakes IN LOVE

Snakes are famously desirable and attractive. They make for sensual romantic partners, too. In love, Snakes require a companion who is in touch not only with their physical passion but also their emotional and mental intelligence.

Snakes are wise and require stimulation across all their senses otherwise they may slip away silently. Although Snakes appear calm and cool on the surface, underneath their skin burns an intensity that can lead to vanity, selfishness and a sharp tongue.

Thankfully, their bark is worse than their bite.

PERFECT MATCH

In love, Snakes don't play too nicely with Tigers or Pigs as they are deemed too reckless or straightforward for wise and pensive Snakes.

The perfect match for Snakes are Oxen, Roosters and Monkeys, offering a playful but stable counter to the seriously straight Snake.

For deep and fulfilling relationships, Snakes pair nicely with Horses, Dragons and Goats.

snakes AT WORK

Snakes are solitary, independent creatures. They prefer not to rely on other people unless they absolutely need to.

This also applies to the workplace. Snakes are cynical of other people's judgement and abilities, meaning they inspect and examine the work of others. Thankfully, Snakes possess great wisdom, so they are usually proved right when others are proved wrong.

Complex problems also stimulate Snakes, allowing them to be excellent problem-solvers and thrive under tight deadlines.

snakes in their ELEMENT

Wood Snake (1965, 2025)
Creative, flexible, compassionate

Fire Snake (1977, 2037)
Passionate, communicative, enthusiastic

Earth Snake (1929, 1989)
Practical, reliable, responsible

Metal Snake (1941, 2001)
Determined, resilient, ambitious

Water Snake (1953, 2013)
Sensitive, insightful, perceptive

the GREAT RACE

Aware of its limitations in speed and strength, the Snake created a clever strategy during the Great Race.

It coiled itself around the Horse's hoof and let the Horse carry it across the river towards the finish line.

There, at the last moment, the Snake uncoiled – startling and slowing the Horse – and slithered across the finish line ahead of the Horse.

This tactic showcased not only the Snake's wisdom but also its indolence.

NOTABLE snakes

Brooke Shields, 1965

Bob Dylan, 1941

Daniel Radcliffe, 1989

Robert Downey Jr, 1965

Richard Dawkins, 1941

Taylor Swift, 1989

Audrey Hepburn, 1929

Billie Eilish, 2001

John F. Kennedy, 1917

J. K. Rowling, 1965

snakes in their
OWN WORDS

"Life is short. Have adventures."

Taylor Swift
interview with Zara Irshad, *San Francisco Chronicle*, December 7, 2023.

"Listen, smile, agree and then do whatever you were gonna do anyway."

Robert Downey Jr
Inside the Actors Studio,
September 7, 2006.

YIN and YANG

find your yin...

Yin and Yang are concepts from ancient Chinese philosophy that describe how opposite forces in the world are interconnected with each other in a complementary way.

In Chinese culture, Yin and Yang are applied in various ways in the East, including medicine, martial arts, feng shui and philosophy. When Yin and Yang come together, the world is in a beautiful state of balance and harmony.

...find your yang

happy NEW YEAR

Chinese New Year, also known as the Lunar New Year or Spring Festival, falls on different dates each year because it is based on the lunar calendar. The date of the new year falls on the second new moon after the winter solstice on December 21. Generally, this occurs between January 21 and February 20. This also means that the Chinese zodiac year can begin from February.

HORSE

elegant and energetic

year of the horse:
1930, 1942, 1954, 1966,
1978, 1990, 2002, 2014,
2026, 2038

chinese word: **MĂ**

motto: **I RUN FREE**

yin/yang: **YANG**

season: **SUMMER**

lunar month: **JUNE -JULY**

ruling hour: **11:00 -12:59**

western zodiac: **GEMINI**

positive qualities: elegant, sporty, sociable

negative qualities: self-centred, impulsive, over-confident

Horses are on their feet around the clock to showcase their strong work ethic and endurance.

They are also energetic, free-spirited and sociable, with strong communication skills and a love of adventure. They also thrive on running wild towards new experiences.

ARE YOU a horse?

You can be playful, silly and funny when you've got nothing to do, and hardworking and focused when there's important work to be done.

Most things come easy due to your natural power and athleticism and you love to keep yourself active.

You can be a little self-centred sometimes, but you're a Horse: you don't like to be tied down to others.

the LUCK of the horse

lucky

numbers: 2, 3 and 7

days: 5th and 20th

colours: yellow, green

flowers: calla lily, jasmine

unlucky

numbers: 1, 5 and 6

colours: blue, white

horses IN LOVE

Horses look for a romantic partner as silly, adventurous and carefree as they are. They search for someone who is independent, loyal, spontaneous and just as keen to roam wild and free alongside them.

A Horse understands the value of commitment but refuses to be reined in or tethered to someone else's ideals.

A Horse loves human connection and intimacy and is can be too gentle and soft-hearted.

PERFECT MATCH

Horses fall in love easily. It's part of their curious and adventurous spirit.

Luckily, they're strong enough to pick themselves up when relationships fail. That's a power only Horses have. Horses fall deepest with Dogs, Tigers and Goats.

The traits of these animals – loyalty, adventurousness and gentleness – harmonize with a Horse. For friendship, Horses tend to enjoy the company of Snakes, Rabbits and Dragons the most. Rats and Oxen – stay away. Your deception and seriousness are not courses that Horses wish to be served.

horses AT WORK

Horses play hard as much as they work hard. And a Horse won't quit until a job is finished. They can multitask better than most, employing their intelligence, strength and endurance all at once.

Horses make great colleagues, too – extroverted individuals who thrive in professional settings as much as social ones.

A Horse's flaw? Sometimes, they can run wild and their impulsiveness can lead them into hot water.

Occasionally, a little reigning in is required.

horses in their ELEMENT

Wood Horse (1954, 2014)
Sentimental, imaginative, insightful

Fire Horse (1966, 2026)
Charismatic, lively, stubborn

Earth Horse (1978, 2038)
Kind-hearted, righteous, irritable

Metal Horse (1930, 1990)
Straightforward, calm, rational

Water Horse (1942, 2002)
Reliable, amicable, charming

the GREAT RACE

The Horse galloped towards the finish line of the Great Race with overwhelming confidence and swam vigorously across the mighty river.

However, as the Horse approached the finish line, the Snake, which had been coiled around the Horse's hoof, scared the Horse so much it slowed down to a gentle trot.

It came seventh, and, of course, it forgave the Snake.

NOTABLE horses

Nelson Mandela, 1918

Emma Watson, 1990

Paul McCartney, 1942

Joe Biden, 1942

Clint Eastwood, 1930

Jackie Chan, 1954

Margot Robbie, 1990

Jimi Hendrix, 1942

Kobe Bryant, 1978

Gordon Ramsay, 1966

horses in their
OWN WORDS

"I am the master of my fate, I am the captain of my soul."

Nelson Mandela
from his favourite poem "Invictus" by William Ernest Henley (which he often recited to fellow prisoners while he was incarcerated), 1875.

"The measure of a man wasn't how many times or how hard he got knocked down, but how fast he got back up."

Joe Biden

Promises to Keep, 2008.

earthly RULING HOURS

Ancient Chinese cultures were the first civilizations on Earth to observe that the moon had **12 lunar cycles** that could rotate to 12 months in a solar year.

They were also the first to divide the day and night into 12 hours.

Each animal of the Chinese zodiac was then gifted with one hour of the day. These are called **earthly ruling hours**.

It is believed that during these hours, animal signs are at their most powerful.

"It does not matter how slowly you go so long as you do not stop."

Confucius
The Analects, Chapter 1, 4th century BC.

GOAT

stable and friendly

year of the goat:
1931, 1943, 1955, 1967,
1979, 1991, 2003, 2015,
2027, 2039

chinese word: **YÁNG**

motto: **I CARE**

yin/yang: **YIN**

season: **SUMMER**

lunar month: **JULY – AUGUST**

ruling hour: **13:00 – 14:59**

western zodiac: **CANCER**

positive qualities: nurturing, gentle, team player

negative qualities: pessimistic, short-sighted, follower

In the Chinese zodiac, the Goat, also known as the Sheep or the Ram, is a symbol of kindness, gentleness and peace. It is known to favour the spiritual over the material and is the most tender and mild of all the zodiac animal signs.

ARE YOU a goat?

You can be reserved, quiet and shy, but there's a lot more to you.

You can be as tough as nails when you want to be, with an indelible sense of duty to do whatever is needed to protect your family and friends.

As a goat, you're creative without the pretence, content with being artistic simply for your own entertainment.

You can be pessimistic and cynical – even a little melancholic – but it helps keep you grounded. You are the most stable person you know, after all.

the LUCK of the goat

lucky

numbers: 2 and 7

days: 7th and 30th

colours: brown, red, purple

flowers: carnations, primroses

unlucky

numbers: 4 and 9

colours: blue, black

goats IN LOVE

Goats are not looking for thrills and rollercoaster romances.

They seek someone who treats people the same as they treat others – with support, tenderness and empathy.

Goats are beloved for their ability to listen and understand, and they place a strong focus on upholding family values and creating stable emotional roots.

PERFECT MATCH

Goats fall in love easily with Rabbits, Pigs and Horses as they are bound together by the same traits of decency, compassion and generosity.

However, Rats are incompatible with Goats – they can be too devious for a friendly Goat.

goats AT WORK

Goats are the ultimate team players.

They are not concerned with individual status and power. Intuitive and sensitive to the needs of others in the workplace, Goats are well equipped to provide support, comfort and counsel to junior members of a team, and they are also stable and experienced enough to lead.

However, a Goat's indecisiveness and tendency to avoid confrontation means they are not capable of always making tough decisions when they are necessary.

goats in their ELEMENT

Wood Goat (1955, 2015)
Gentle, compassionate, friendly

Fire Goat (1967, 2027)
Frank, honest, meticulous

Earth Goat (1979, 2039)
Righteous, intuitive, indecisive

Metal Goat (1931, 1991)
Ambitious, kind-hearted, stubborn

Water Goat (1943, 2003)
Supportive, helpful, nurturing

the GREAT RACE

Slow and doubtful of its own abilities, the Goat was unlikely to ever win the Great Race. Knowing this, the Goat suggested that the Monkey and the Rooster work together to increase their chances of success.

When they reached the mighty river, together they found a raft and used it to cross the water. The Rooster steered, the Monkey pushed and the Goat led the way by shouting directions. Through their combined efforts, they crossed the river successfully.

At the finish line, the Monkey and the Rooster let the Goat finish first out of respect for its teamwork.

NOTABLE goats

Julia Roberts, 1967

Steve Jobs, 1955

Chris Pratt, 1979

Olivia Rodrigo, 2003

Ed Sheeran, 1991

Frida Kahlo, 1907

P!nk, 1979

Kurt Cobain, 1967

George Harrison, 1943

William Shatner, 1931

goats in their
OWN WORDS

"It's possible that the universe exists only for me. If so, it's sure going well for me, I must admit."

Bill Gates

Time magazine, January 13, 1997.

"Your work is going to fill a large part of your life, and the only way to be truly satisfied is to do what you believe is great work. And the only way to do great work is to love what you do."

Steve Jobs

Stanford Commencement Address, June 12, 2005.

MONKEY

entertaining and cheeky

year of the monkey:
1932, 1944, 1956, 1968,
1980, 1992, 2004, 2016,
2028, 2040

chinese word: **HÓU**

motto: **I PLAY**

yin/yang: **YANG**

season: **AUTUMN**

lunar month: **AUGUST– SEPTEMBER**

ruling hour: **15:00–16:59**

western zodiac: **LEO**

positive qualities: high-spirited, social, curious

negative qualities: mischievous, manipulative, easily bored

Creative, curious and cheeky, the Monkey's place in the zodiac is unique.

While it possesses little of the physical strength or resourcefulness of other animals, the Monkey succeeds by surviving on its mischievous wits and magnetic personality.

ARE YOU a monkey?

Monkeys are the jokers of the pack. You can be highly sociable and revel in showing off your social climbing skills, charm and emotional intelligence.

You can be quick to learn and adapt to new people and places, and you love a challenge – though you're just as good at wriggling out of one if you don't want to do it.

You can be mischievous and tend to exploit and manipulate others. This can often get you in trouble, but, luckily, you're charming enough to get out of that, too.

the LUCK of the monkey

lucky

numbers: 4 and 9

days: 4th and 14th

colours: white, blue, gold

flower: chrysanthemum

unlucky

numbers: 2 and 7

colours: red, pink

monkeys IN LOVE

Everybody loves a cheeky, albeit slightly naughty, Monkey. And romantic partners are no different. Monkeys are spontaneous and positive, with a heightened sense of humour, but they can get easily bored if no one laughs with them. Monkeys tend to be the most commitment-phobic of all the astrological animals as their playfulness lends itself to promiscuity.

All work and no play sends the Monkey away, after all. However, once Monkeys find the perfect partner, they commit in every possible way. Since Monkeys are sociable and love to talk, it's easy to relate to them.

PERFECT MATCH

Monkeys are friends with everyone, but they match especially well with Dogs, Oxen, Roosters and Rabbits.

In love, a Monkey's ultimate partner tends to be a Dragon, Rat or Snake – they're devious, magical and attractive enough to keep the attention of a fickle Monkey.

Monkeys and Tigers fight too much, and sincere Pigs should stay well clear of any Monkey business.

monkeys AT WORK

In the Chinese zodiac, Monkeys represent flexibility. And flexible people usually make great leaders.

Monkeys are also known for being erratic geniuses, easily solving the most difficult problems. Unfortunately, Monkeys are also people pleasers – entertainers – and have a habit of being too agreeable. If they can't do what they want, they become bored and discouraged.

Highly successful and well liked, Monkeys can always be found at the top of any tree and corporate ladder.

monkeys
in their ELEMENT

Wood Monkey (1944, 2004)
Helpful, compassionate, stubborn

Fire Monkey (1956, 2016)
Ambitious, adventurous, irritable

Earth Monkey (1968, 2028)
Frank, optimistic, fearless

Metal Monkey (1980, 2040)
Smart, quick-witted, stubborn

Water Monkey (1932, 1992)
Smart, quick-witted, fond of attention

the GREAT RACE

The Jade Emperor presumed that the nimble and quick Monkey would be a front-runner to win the Great Race.

Alas, as the race progressed, the Monkey could not find a way to swing across the mighty river, so he teamed up with the Goat and the Rooster.

Together, they used a raft to navigate the river safely. The Monkey used its limber limbs to row the raft while the Rooster steered and the Goat led the way.

NOTABLE monkeys

Tom Hanks, 1956

Kim Kardashian, 1980

Ryan Gosling, 1980

Daniel Craig, 1968

Millie Bobby Brown, 2004

Charlie Chaplin, 1920

Will Smith, 1968

Céline Dion, 1968

Elizabeth Taylor, 1972

Sofía Vergara, 1972

monkeys in their
OWN WORDS

"I didn't start as anything close to a diva. I don't know that you get anything extra without being human first."

Kylie Minogue
interview with Brittany Spanos, *Rolling Stone*,
September 11, 2023.

"I am what I am: an individual, unique and different, with a lineal history of an ancestral promptings and urgings, a history of dreams, desires and of special experiences, of all of which I am the sum total."

Charlie Chaplin
My Autobiography, 1964.

FAN TAI SUI

According to ancient Chinese astrology, a person's birth sign year – once every 12 years – brings only **bad luck**.

It is in your birth year that Tai Sui, the God of Age, burdens you with his curse – a whole year of misfortune – as you have offended him by growing older.

Followers of the zodiac offer Tai Sui sacrifices and prayers in the hope of increasing their blessings in their zodiac year.

"Luck is what happens when preparation meets opportunity."

Seneca the Younger
4 CE.

ROOSTER

entertaining and cheeky

year of the rooster:
1933, 1945, 1957, 1969,
1981, 1993, 2005, 2017,
2029, 2041

chinese word: JĪ

motto: I AM RESILIENT

yin/yang: YIN

season: AUTUMN

lunar month: SEPTEMBER – OCTOBER

ruling hour: 17:00 – 18:59

western zodiac: VIRGO

positive qualities: efficient,
methodical, assertive

negative qualities: arrogant,
outspoken, selfish

Often regarded as a symbol of perseverance
and resilience in Chinese astrology, the
Rooster is famed for its punctuality, ambition
and assertiveness.

As the loudest of all spirit animals, the
Rooster naturally loves the sound of its
own voice.

ARE YOU a rooster?

You can be capable, devoted and observant. You hate to fail yourself and others.

You can be eccentric, selfish and outspoken but it's rarely off-putting as you're only being honest.

You enjoy the spotlight and will step into it whatever chance you get.

Thankfully, you're attractive to look at so people don't mind it when you hog all the attention!

the LUCK of the rooster

lucky

numbers: 5, 7 and 8

days: 5th and 7th

colours: gold, brown, yellow

flowers: gladiolus, cockscomb

unlucky

numbers: 1, 3 and 9

colour: red

roosters IN LOVE

Roosters are loyal partners who value fidelity, honesty and sincerity.

They are dedicated and supportive, too, offering a tower of stability, efficiency and responsibility in relationships.

That may not make the Rooster sound sexy and romantic to many, but to the wild and carefree, a Rooster can be a comforting and safe place to hang their hat.

PERFECT MATCH

Rabbits and Dogs are not a Rooster's best friend, so those relationships are best avoided.

However, a Rooster always meets his best match in an Ox, Snake and Dragon, largely due to the fact they are all beautiful and attractive creatures. (And Roosters love flattery, don't they?)

roosters AT WORK

Roosters dislike criticism, even though they are quick to find fault with others in the workplace. This can often alienate colleagues.

Roosters make great freelancers – they are punctual, organized and detail-oriented enough to get the work done on their own time.

Roosters revel in roles that require precision and efficiency. Roosters command – and demand – attention in social settings, so you'll always remember a Rooster on the morning after a Christmas party.

roosters in their ELEMENT

Wood Rooster (1945, 2005)
Energetic, tender, unstable

Fire Rooster (1957, 2017)
Trustworthy, punctual, responsible

Earth Rooster (1969, 2029)
Loving, generous, trustworthy

Metal Rooster (1921, 1981)
Determined, brave, perseverant

Water Rooster (1933, 1993)
Smart, quick-witted, compassionate

the GREAT RACE

Despite their confidence to the contrary, the Rooster was never likely to win the Great Race. Thankfully, the Goat suggested joining forces with the Monkey and the Rooster to cross the mighty river.

Using their combined skills, the trio worked together to cross the river safely on a raft.

The Rooster played the crucial role of steering the raft. The Monkey provided the forward momentum, and the Goat provided directions. Teamwork made the dream work.

NOTABLE roosters

Beyoncé, 1981

Ariana Grande, 1993

Jay-Z, 1969

Michael Caine, 1933

Serena Williams, 1981

Prince Philip, 1921

Jennifer Lopez, 1969

Chris Evans, 1981

Britney Spears, 1981

Yoko Ono, 1933

roosters in their
OWN WORDS

"Power is not given to you.
You have to take it."

Beyoncé
interview with *ELLE*, December 2019.

"I'm smart about who I am.
I know what I can, can't, will
and won't do, and if I have to be
strict about that, I will."

Dolly Parton

interview with *Rolling Stone*, October 30,
2003.

DOG

protective and loyal

year of the dog:
1934, 1946, 1958, 1970,
1982, 1994, 2006, 2018,
2030, 2042

chinese word: **GǑU**

motto: **I AM LOYAL**

yin/yang: **YANG**

season: **AUTUMN**

lunar month: **OCTOBER – NOVEMBER**

ruling hour: **19:00 – 20:59**

western zodiac: **LIBRA**

positive qualities: devoted, caring, obedient

negative qualities: cynical, critical, careless

A man's best friend, the Dog is the most faithful of all the spirit animals in the Chinese zodiac, happy to bound into people's lives with an energy, enthusiasm and integrity that knows no limits.

ARE YOU a dog?

Dogs possess the greatest traits of human nature – loyalty and honesty. And these are the two traits that you take most seriously in yourself and others.

You can be fiercely friendly, faithful, dependable and protective.

You can be a bit careless, over-sensitive and grumpy, but you also go to great lengths to gain everybody's trust and respect without expecting it back.

In short: you are the perfect life companion.

the LUCK of the dog

lucky

numbers: 3, 4 and 9

days: 7th and 28th

colours: red, green, purple

flowers: rose, cymbidium orchids

unlucky

numbers: 1, 6 and 7

colours: blue, white, gold

dogs IN LOVE

Dogs put their family first. They put down strong roots and seek to find a romantic partner who shares those values.

A Dog also demands tenderness, so any lovers or friends must exude affection and intimacy. Daily hugs are a must.

Dogs are great listeners, too, making them the best of friends with talkative Rats.

Dogs need constant reassurance and can be a bit clingy, but as long as they are allowed to be silly, play games and sleep in, they are easy to please.

PERFECT MATCH

Dogs match perfectly with Tigers, Horses and Rabbits.

They complement their sense of adventure, honesty and vulnerability.

Dogs can get excitable, so they require regular high jinks with Monkeys and Pigs to let off steam. Dogs don't sit well with Dragons and Roosters, so these two animals are best avoided.

dogs AT WORK

Dogs are the ideal employees and make for obedient and helpful followers.

They are warm and friendly and work hard for the person they think is most important.

They're not always diligent in their work – their brains get easily overwhelmed – and they lack communication skills as they find it difficult to express their thoughts.

As Dogs can get easily distracted, they aren't terribly good at keeping to deadlines.

dogs in their ELEMENT

Wood Dog (1934, 1994)
Friendly, cooperative, empathetic

Fire Dog (1946, 2006)
Energetic, passionate, courageous

Earth Dog (1958, 2018)
Practical, reliable, hardworking

Metal Dog (1970, 2030)
Determined, disciplined, ambitious

Water Dog (1922, 1982)
Intelligent, adaptable, communicative

the GREAT RACE

Naturally, the eager Dog couldn't wait for the Great Race to begin.

As the race progressed, the Dog grew distracted, stopping to splash and play in the mighty river. It prioritized having fun over winning.

This showcases a Dog's playful nature and lack of concentration.

NOTABLE dogs

Michael Jackson, 1958

Donald Trump, 1946

Mother Teresa, 1910

Justin Bieber, 1994

Harry Styles, 1994

Christopher Nolan, 1970

Judi Dench, 1934

Nicki Minaj, 1982

Freddie Mercury, 1946

Brigitte Bardot, 1934

dogs in their
OWN WORDS

"Love begins at home, and it is not how much we do, but how much love we put in the action that we do."

Mother Teresa
Nobel Peace Prize lecture, 1979.

"The most important thing is
to live a fabulous life. As long as it's
fabulous, I don't care how long
it is."

Freddie Mercury

PIG

generous and easy-going

year of the pig:
1935, 1947, 1959, 1971,
1983, 1995, 2007, 2019,
2031, 2043

chinese word: **ZHŪ**

motto: **I AM EAGER**

yin/yang: **YIN**

season: **AUTUMN**

lunar month: **NOVEMBER – DECEMBER**

ruling hour: **21:00 – 22:59**

western zodiac: **SCORPIO**

positive qualities: considerate, unpretentious, cheerful

negative qualities: naive, self-indulgent, lazy

Last but not least, the Pig was the final animal to cross the finishing line in the Jade Emperor's Great Race.

While Pigs may sometimes be considered lazy, of all the animals in the zodiac, they are in fact the most content within themselves.

Have you ever seen a sad Pig?

ARE YOU a pig?

You can be optimistic and easy-going.

You love to laugh and play games and don't care about being seen as cool or popular. It comes naturally to you.

You don't like to argue, you're happy to back down even when you know you're right and you will selflessly put the needs of others before your own.

You don't mind making a mess, which others may find annoying, but your defence is simple: life is too short to tidy up.

the LUCK of the pig

lucky

numbers: 2, 5 and 8

days: 7th and 24th

colours: yellow, grey, brown, gold

flowers: hydrangea, daisy

unlucky

numbers: 1 and 7

colours: red, blue, green

pigs IN LOVE

Pigs can be a little too trusting at times – maybe even naive – and that gullibility can make Pigs vulnerable to exploitation.

Because Pigs are caring, generous and out-going, they require a partner who provides companionship, physical intimacy and emotional security to complement their key values.

Put simply: Pigs are looking for someone who will roll around in the mud with them without complaining about the smell.

PERFECT MATCH

Pigs fall in love easily. Not always a good thing, especially when Pigs can be so trusting so quick.

Pigs should stay clear of the selfish – listen up, Snakes and Monkeys! – as they can be easily manipulated by charm and beauty.

A Pig's perfect match could be an adventurous Tiger, a devoted Rabbit or a sensitive Goat.

pigs AT WORK

Pigs have mastered the art of concentration, so they are supremely effective in the workplace.

A determined and diligent Pig has a strong sense of responsibility for their workload and will devote all their energy to achieving their goals.

Like their position in the Great Race, a Pig will be the last to leave the office every night.

pigs in their # ELEMENT

Wood Pig (1935, 1995)
Friendly, cooperative, compassionate

Fire Pig (1947, 2007)
Passionate, energetic, outgoing

Earth Pig (1959, 2019)
Practical, reliable, hardworking

Metal Pig (1971, 2031)
Determined, disciplined, ambitious

Water Pig (1923, 1983)
Intelligent, adaptable, communicative

the GREAT RACE

The Pig came last in the Great Race. It set off with determination but soon found itself distracted… by food, of course! During the race, the Pig stopped to eat, rest, eat and rest again, enjoying every opportunity to indulge.

The Pig made its way slowly and steadily to the finishing line, taking advantage of its natural swimming ability to cross the mighty river, no matter how full its stomach was.

The Pig's journey showcases its qualities of determination, resilience and the ability to enjoy life's pleasures while still achieving its goals.

NOTABLE pigs

Dua Lipa, 1995

Arnold Schwarzenegger, 1947

Henry Cavill, 1983

Elon Musk, 1971

Elton John, 1947

Amy Winehouse, 1983

Snoop Dogg, 1971

Timothée Chalamet, 1995

Hugh Laurie, 1959

Ginger Rogers, 1911

pigs in their
OWN WORDS

"It's OK to have your eggs in one basket, as long as you control what happens to that basket."

Elon Musk
interview with *Inc. Magazine*, 2007.

"I don't care what people think about me. Never did, never will. Life is too short to be worrying about that."

Amy Winehouse
Interview magazine, August 2007.

Red is considered the luckiest colour in Chinese culture. By wearing the colour in your birth year – along with jade accessories – you can ward off bad fortune and evil spirits sent by Tai Sui, the God of Age.

However, in order for the luck of the red colour to drive away misfortune, the items of clothing must be bought for you by a partner, family member or friend.

> "As a colour, red represents so many things – power, sensuality, vulnerability and strength."
>
> **Zadrian Smith**
> *Vogue*, December 8, 2021.